101 GREATEST
MAGIC SECRETS

EXPOSED

Herbert L. Becker

CITADEL PRESS
Kensington Publishing Corp.
http://www.kensingtonbooks.com

CITADEL PRESS BOOKS are published by

Kensington Publishing Corp.
850 Third Avenue
New York, NY 10022

Copyright © 2002 Herbert L. Becker

All Kensington titles, imprints, and distributed lines are available at special quantity discounts for bulk purchases for sales promotions, premiums, fund-raising, educational, or institutional use. Special book excerpts or customized printings can also be created to fit specific needs. For details, write or phone the office of the Kensington special sales manager: Kensington Publishing Corp., 850 Third Avenue, New York, NY 10022, attn: Special Sales Department, phone 1-800-221-2647.

Citadel Press and the Citadel Logo are trademarks of Kensington Publishing Corp.

First Citadel printing: March 2002

10 9 8 7 6 5 4 3 2 1

Printed in the United States of America

Cataloging data may be obtained from the Library of Congress

ISBN 0-8065-2154-6

To my six wonderful children:

Randi, *who at twenty years of age should be reminded that she can still dream about becoming a Fairy Princess.*

Adam, *who is striving to become the next Ray Bradbury.*

Brian, *who loves to illustrate. Many of his illustrations are in this book.*

Gillah, *who loves to dance and put on shabbos shows.*

Dovid, *who always wants to "talk about things."*

Nechemiah, *who at two years of age, finds everything to be magical.*

And to all of us who wish to harness a little magic solely for the enjoyment of themselves and others.

Special thanks to my editor Hillel Black
for his editorial magic,
to David Copperfield and Andre Kole
for their advice and suggestions,
and most of all, thanks to my wife
for putting up with the long hours
it takes to write a book.

Contents

Part Two—Hypnotic Hijinks: The Dunninger Hypnotism Act

Part Three—Rope and Knot Tricks

Author to Reader

What do magic and crossword puzzles have in common? Both are puzzles and people like to solve them. In this book, I will offer the solutions to some of the world's most guarded magic secrets. Most likely, you will not be headlining in Vegas anytime soon. Nevertheless, you have the right to be curious about the amazing magic tricks that professional magicians perform, and I think you also have the right to know how they are done. I will unveil to you the secrets of magic's most famous magicians.

The advanced magic of today possesses a fascination that can only be fully appreciated by those who have some knowledge of the art itself. Increasing interest in the subject has demanded a book, ranging from simpler, individually performed tricks to those requiring special apparatus, custom props, a staff of accomplices, and/or the larger venue of the full-service magic stage.

In covering many aspects of the magic business, *101 Magic Secrets Exposed* will provide the reader with great learning tools, not just an exposé of magic. I'll also describe the skill, ingenuity, and showmanship required in the profession, something that has too often been neglected in books on magic. To do so in an entertaining and explicit way, I have included explanations of the incredible illusory effects produced by the world's most famous magicians.

Today, more than ever, artistry and stage presence stand as the real test of a magician's ability to please the public. Magic itself has long since ceased to be a secret craft. Answer an advertisement in popular hobby magazines and you will get a deluge of catalogs from magic dealers who offer practically anything you can imagine at prices ranging from as little as one dollar to thousands, with no restrictions on the buyer. In other words, you do not have to be a member of a magic club or secret society in order to purchase magic tricks.

Elaborate novelty and magic shops display their merchandise in most cities, and they are open to all customers. A magician recently told me that Tannen's Magic Shop of New York City sells tricks to anyone—meaning that you do not have to be a professional magician to buy the pros' tricks and gain their trade secrets. So much for the old fantasy of some confidential "secret code of magicians." Magic retailers flourish alongside novelty dealers, luring purchasers with window displays of attractively priced magical apparatus. Today, anyone can learn the methods of magic, trick by trick. To become as proficient as a professional magician, the amateur needs only to study the tricks and practice performing them in larger and larger venues until his or her name appears in lights.

I hope this book will mark another important step in the advancement of popular magical literature. I am not exposing the weaknesses of magicians; I am revealing their strengths. This book has been written with a spirit of respect and admiration for the great men and women of magic whose methods are described within these pages. An art form is only as great as the innovative people who create within it, and the artistic mastery of the great magical personalities should be shared with every newcomer to the craft.

101 GREATEST
MAGIC SECRETS
EXPOSED

PART ONE

CARD TRICKS

1

SVENGALI DECK

*A deck of different cards magically changes into
a deck of the same card, the chosen card.*

*E*very magician must have this trick. A deck of playing cards is
riffled. At a spectator's command the magician stops the riffle. The
deck will be cut at this point, revealing the card chosen by the
spectator. (While the magician was riffling, it was evident that
the deck contained many cards.) Once the spectator has seen the
chosen card, it is placed on the bottom of the deck. The deck is
again riffled, now all the cards have changed into the one chosen
by the spectator. The chosen card is removed from the bottom and
placed on the top. The deck is riffled again, and now it is back to a
normal deck with different cards.

THE SECRET:

Every other card is the same. Twenty-six cards are different;
twenty-six cards are the same. The twenty-six "same" cards are
slightly shorter than the twenty-six other cards. When you riffle in
one direction, the short card falls with the long one, revealing the
deck as a regular deck. When riffled in the opposite direction, the

long cards are held back and the short cards are the only ones seen. The deck appears to be one card.

This is pretty much all this deck can do. Each time you show the trick, the same card will be the "only" card in the deck. While you can make the chosen card show up on the top, or the middle, or the bottom, you are still dealing with a single card. People will catch on if spectators always choose the same card. Of course, you could have the deck divided into three short cards. The first third of the deck would have the two of clubs as the short card, the next third could be the jack of spades, and the last third would be the four of diamonds.

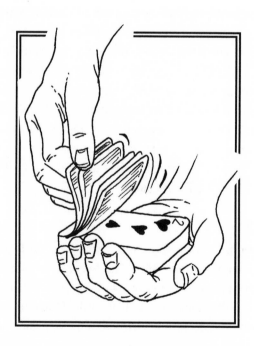

2
STRIPPER DECK

A mechanical deck helps locate chosen cards.

*M*uch like the Svengali deck, this is a "trick" deck. It has been manufactured so that it is tapered on one end. When all the cards are stacked together and aligned, the taper is not noticed. When a card is reversed in the deck, it will be easy to find since the card will protrude at the narrow end of the deck. The deck, in its simplest form, is used to locate chosen cards. A card is chosen at random from the deck, and before the card is returned to the deck, the magician turns the deck around. Now that the card is protruding, it will be easy for the magician to find it.

A TRICK TO PERFORM WITH THIS DECK:

Shuffle the cards, then spread them facedown on the table. Ask that a card be slid out of the deck. Square up the deck while the card is being inspected. Have the chosen card slid back into the deck. Hand out your business card and ask that the name of the chosen card be written on the back of the business card (see item A). Shuffle the deck and place it on the table (see item B). Have the business card placed on top of the deck. Square the deck. Now cut the deck a few more times. Have the deck cut to the location of the business card. The chosen card will be directly under this card. This is a simple trick mechanically, but it does take a little flair from the magician.

Item A: Once the card has been chosen, reverse the deck as you square it up. Allow the spectator to slip the card back into the deck. Do a few overhand shuffles as the name of the chosen card is written on your business card.

Item B: While you are shuffling, you must find the reversed card, which is protruding at one end of the deck. Work it to the top of the deck. This is done by keeping track of the reversed card while you continue mixing the deck. When the business card is placed on top of the deck, it is being placed upon the chosen card. Make mention of how you have shuffled the deck, then shuffle some more. While you are shuffling, ask if the card has been memorized. Mention how the card and now the business card are hopelessly mixed into the deck. Tell them how impossible it would be to keep track of the card or the business card.

Place the deck down and ask that it be cut to the location of the business card. Remove the business card, announce the name of the chosen card written on it, then have the top card turned over. Let them keep your business card (good for business) and remain mum on the secret.

This is good for meeting people at trade shows, restaurants, or bars. You present your business card in a memorable way which breaks the ice and gets a conversation started.

Although mostly magicians use this trick, salespeople could make good use of it, too.

3

MENE TECKLE DECK

The selected card appears on the top of the deck.

 S trange name, good deck. The secret to this deck is the fact that it is made up of twenty-six different pairs of cards, for a total of fifty-two cards, and it can be purchased at most magic shops. One of the cards in each pair is a millimeter shorter than its mate. The shorter card is on top of the longer one. When the cards are riffled, the two cards fall as one. To the audience it appears to be a regular deck of cards.

THE TRICK:

Riffle the deck and have someone insert a finger into the deck, or simply tell you to stop. Cut the cards at this point. Show the top card or have the spectator slip this card off the top of the deck. Once the card has been seen, place it or have it slipped into the deck. Since this card was one of two identical cards, its mate remains on the top of the deck after the chosen card has been slipped back into the deck. Pick up the deck, give it a tap, and the chosen card has seemingly moved from within the deck to reappear on the top.

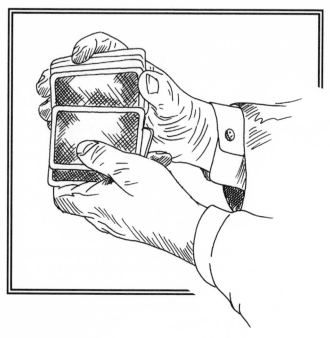

ANOTHER TRICK:

Riffle the deck and have the audience member pick the point where you are to stop either by inserting a finger or by calling out "Stop!" Cut the deck at this point and place the deck on a table. Have the audience member slip the top card off the deck. Pick up the rest of the deck and have the chosen card returned to it. Then ask, "What card did you choose?" Count the numeric value of the chosen card onto a pile from the deck. In other words, if they chose an ace, count that as one; a two of diamonds (or whatever suit) would be two cards; etc. (a jack is eleven, a queen is twelve, and a king is thirteen).

When you count the cards off the top of the deck, the mate of the chosen card would be the first card removed from the top of the deck. Once counted out, it becomes the bottom card of the counted pile. Pick up this pile and recount the cards. Now the top card is the mate of the one chosen. Turn this card over, and the chosen card has appeared in a magical way.

This trick deck has some good points and some bad ones. You can do both of these tricks for the same audience at one sitting with little chance that the deck will get out of order. As you may recall, the shorter card is resting on its longer, identical mate. This is a big advantage over the Svengali deck. However, more than two tricks might prove to be too much of a risk. Each time you put a card back into the deck you not only break up the pair that consists of the chosen card and its mate, you also break up whichever pair happens to be at the point where the chosen card has been replaced into the deck. Broken pairs make this deck useless.

4

ONE-HAND PASS

A simple way to force a card on a spectator

You hold a deck of cards in your left hand (I am a righty, so I use my left hand). With a slick move, sometimes called the Charlier pass, the deck is cut. A card is selected from the cut deck. The deck is squared up and the magician instantly names the chosen card.

THE SECRET:

This pass (or cut) is a method of secretly cutting the deck so that a selected card may be brought at once from the top of the deck to the middle. To the audience, it appears that the deck has been fairly cut and a random card has been chosen. In fact, the top card has been brought to the center of the cut. Hold the cards face-down in your left hand. (Take note of the top card beforehand.) The deck is held lengthwise, supported between the thumb on one side and the fingers on the other. Release a little pressure from your thumb and let half the deck fall into your palm.

With the forefinger, slide the bottom section in your palm up along the upright section that is still being held in place with your thumb. If you continue to push this section up, over the tip of the cards being held by your thumb, at the point where the palmed section will replace the section that was being held in place by your thumb, an exchange will happen. The section that was held by your thumb is now lying across your fingers and into your palm. Your thumb now holds up the section that was in your palm.

Confusing? Stick a deck in your hand and try it; it will then make sense.

To the audience, it looks as if you have just done a fancy one-hand cut. In reality, you have cut the deck to the top. An audience member will take this cut-to card; you close and square up the deck. The chosen card is thus the card you saw as the top card. Name the card and the trick is done.

More important, once the card is in the hands of the audience member, you have successfully forced him or her to pick the card you wanted chosen—the top card.

Simply naming the card will reveal your magic powers. However, why stop there? Make a show out of it. Square up the deck and hand it to another member of the audience, turn your back to everyone, and make sure the chosen card is shown to all. Ask that the chosen card be replaced into the deck. Turn back to your audience and tell them that you can locate the card by touch. Have the deck well shuffled, then take the deck and spread it faceup on the table. Look to see if the chosen card is visible; if it is not, spread the cards farther apart until it is. Then tell someone to walk his or her fingers across the deck. When this person goes past the chosen card, ask him or her to stop and walk back. When the selected card is touched, tell the person to stop; this is the chosen card.

By the end of the trick, most people will have forgotten how the chosen card was picked. Great magic.

5

MORE CARD READING

*The magician is able to tell which cards a volunteer
has chosen at random, without seeing them.*

THE SECRET:

Spread a pack of cards on a table faceup and pretend to memorize the whole pack. In reality, you must memorize only the third card from the bottom of the deck. Then stack the cards and spread them out, this time facedown. Ask your volunteer to choose a card. Without looking, you say, hypothetically, "This is the queen of hearts." That is the card you memorized at the beginning, the third card from the bottom. You do not show the card to anyone, but as you pull the card toward you, slightly lift the edge of the card so you can see what it is. Ask the volunteer to choose a second card.

Just as in the previous case, you announce the name of the card that has just been chosen, although neither you nor the audience has seen this card. The card you announce is actually the card that was previously chosen by the spectator. As before, peek at the card, then say now you are going to pick a third card. You pick the third card from the bottom. Without letting anyone look at it, announce what the card is. This time you announce the name of the second card selected. You now have three cards in your hand. No one has seen them yet, but you have somehow announced what they are. Recap your announcements and ask if anyone wants to see the cards in order to verify that you were correct. On the other hand, perhaps they will believe you without seeing the cards. No? Okay, show them the three cards and amaze them with the fact that you were correct. Mix the cards so that when you show them to your audience they will be in a random order so no one will figure out how you did it.

6

Four Aces

*A volunteer will find all four aces. It is a way to get
the volunteer to do the magic.*

A member of the audience chooses a random number of cards
from any pack of cards. The audience member separates these
cards into four piles. When the top card of each stack is revealed,
each is an ace. The rest of the deck is examined in order to prove
that there were only four aces in the deck.

THE SECRET:

Prearrange a pack of cards by placing the four aces on the top.
Put the cards back in the box and put them in your pocket, just so
that you might happen to have a pack on hand at the right moment.

Hand your volunteer the box. Have him or her take the cards
out and make a pile on the table. The pile should be counted out,
one card at a time, facedown onto the table. The stack must con-
sist of more than ten cards. Take back the remaining cards and put
them to one side. Have the volunteer deal the cards into four piles.

Show him or her where you want the piles to be placed. The cards
are dealt to these four piles, one card at a time.

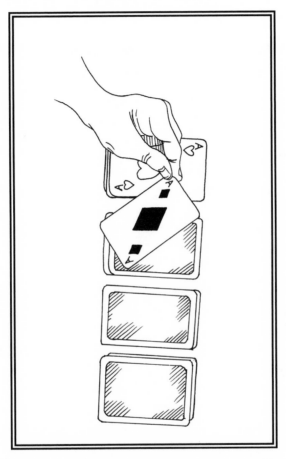

    See to it that all the cards are dealt into the four piles. The four
aces have already been dealt out, one on top of each of the four
piles. Show the audience the four aces and show them that there
are no other aces in the deck.

7

MECHANICAL CARD FIND

The magician will find a card, picked by a helper and randomly replaced in the pack, using a windup toy.

*T*he magician allows a card from any pack of cards to be chosen at random. The deck is mixed and the card is returned. The deck is spread faceup on the table. The magician uses a small windup toy that moves in a straight line to move along the cards and stop at the chosen card.

THE SECRET:

Glance at the bottom card and memorize it. This card is your key card locator. Then spread the cards on the table and let someone choose one card.

Pick up the cards with one hand and with the other hand start dropping and stacking a pile from the top of the pack, until your helper stops you so he can place his card on top of the pile on the table. After he has put his card down you place the rest of the cards on the pile, making sure you have placed the key card locator (the bottom card you sneaked a peek at earlier) on top of your helper's card. Turn the cards over and spread them out. The card you are looking for is the one right after your key card locator. You place the windup toy (with which you have practiced earlier) on the cards. Make sure that it stops on the right card.

It is okay to help the toy along, keeping it on the cards and moving toward the chosen card. When the toy does stop, announce that it has found the chosen card. Since you have practiced with the toy earlier, you know how far it will travel along the cards.

Cut the cards at the point where the toy has stopped and reveal that this is the chosen card, found by a toy.

8

THE AUSTRALIAN SHUFFLE

Mixed-up cards return to their original order.

*T*he magician explains that he has just picked up one of the strangest shuffles he has ever seen; it comes from an Australian casino and is called the Down Under shuffle. The magician shows that he has ten cards in numeric order. A member of the audience is asked to participate, and the shuffle is explained. The spectator then executes the shuffle with complete freedom, as many times as he or she wishes. The cards appear to be completely mixed, but closer inspection proves otherwise!

THE SECRET:

Take from a deck ten cards of one suit from ace to ten. Arrange them in sequence facedown in a pile, the ace being the top card and the ten on the bottom.

Explain to the spectator that the shuffle is from Australia and is called the Down Under shuffle for the following reason: "I will deal the cards onto the table, one at a time. As I lift each card out of my hand, tell me whether you want it to go *down* or *under*. If you ask for the card to go down, I will place it on the table; if you request under, I will place the card under the next top card in my hand and drop them both onto the pile on the table."

If the spectator says down, deal the card in hand down to the table. If the spectator requests under, place the card in your hand under the new top card and drop both to the table.

Continue in this fashion until all the cards have been dealt to the table. Pick up the cards, hand them to the spectator, and request that he or she execute the Down Under shuffle again, dealing the cards down or under as he or she sees fit, with complete freedom of choice.

Offer the spectator the opportunity to repeat the shuffle. (The shuffle can repeated as many times as you wish; the more times it is done the better.) Once the spectator is happy that the cards are shuffled, ask, "Are you completely satisfied that the cards are shuffled and that I couldn't possibly know the order of any of the cards?" Whatever the reply, slowly deal the cards one at a time faceup to the table, naming each card as you deal. They will be in the same order as they were when you started and have not been shuffled at all.

9
Do As I Do

Magician and spectator randomly pick cards from different decks, but each chooses the same card

*T*his trick was used in the film *Magic* starring Anthony Hopkins and is a classic piece of card magic. The magician and the spectator have separate decks of shuffled cards. The spectator is asked to copy every move the magician makes (hence the title of the trick, "Do As I Do"). The magician chooses a card from one pack and the spectator freely chooses a card from the other pack. The outcome is magical and quite startling; both cards match!

THE SECRET:

Start by having two decks of cards, for instance, one red-backed and one blue-backed. Ask the spectator to shuffle both packs and then hand you either pack while keeping the other one for himself or herself. In this example, let us assume he or she hands you the blue deck. Now follow the steps below carefully!

Shuffle your blue deck; make sure the spectator shuffles the red deck. Sneak a glimpse at the bottom card of your deck while shuffling (this is the hardest part of trick, so be careful, do not get spotted). I usually take a glimpse at this card while the spectator is busy; I tilt the bottom of the deck up toward me until I can see the card. Let's say in this instance you spot the ten of clubs; you must remember this card because it is your key card.

Now swap decks with the spectator, place the cards facedown in front of you, making sure the spectator does the same, and say, "I have shuffled the cards that now lie in front of you, and you have shuffled the cards that lie in front of me. Neither of us could know the order of the cards that we now have, is that correct?" (You should now have the red deck, and the spectator should have the blue deck with the key card on the bottom.

Spread your cards in a straight line from left to right, making sure the spectator does the same. Point with your finger about three inches above the spread-out cards at one end and slowly and deliberately move back and forth over the deck, making sure the spectator does the same.

Drop your finger onto the cards (about halfway) and pull out a card. Look at the card, making sure nobody else sees it! However, do not remember this card. It is a bluff! Make sure your spectator takes a card and remembers it. Say the following, "You have had a free choice of a card. Is that correct? Please remember your card."

1. Place your card on top of your spread-out deck, making sure the spectator does the same.
2. Gather up the cards, being careful not to disturb the order. See that the spectator follows your example.
3. Give the deck one complete cut, making sure the spectator does the same.
4. Swap decks. You should now have the blue deck again.

Tell the spectator to find his or her card and place it facedown on the table while you do the same. What you really do is look through the deck and find your key card (in this case, the ten of clubs). The card immediately to the right of it will be the spectator's selection! Take it out and place it facedown on the table.

Try to get your card onto the table first; it looks better. That's it, you are finished! While you are doing the trick, talk about coincidence and free choice. Then get the spectator to turn over his or her card. This builds up the suspense. Then slowly turn over your card!

10

CARD LEVITATION

Magically make cards levitate

*T*he magician explains about gravity and says that if we could defy it we would be able to levitate and possibly even fly. He then proceeds to give a demonstration of being able to do so by placing under his hand a number of playing cards. He slowly lifts his hand from the table and the cards are magically stuck to his hand! He can hold the cards up high for all to see, turn the hand vertically or horizontally, and even shake his hand. The cards remain intact the whole time. Holding his hand above the table, the magician starts to pull the cards away one at a time, and they drop to the table, leaving no clue to how the trick was done.

THE SECRET:

The magician needs to be wearing a ring. A matchstick is placed under the ring so that it comes through and sticks out on either side. Now when you place your hand palm downward on the table you can insert two cards under the hand but above the matchstick. This will give you a solid base for as many cards as you can possibly manage.

You can now lift your hand from the table. If your fingers press down a little on the backs of the cards they will remain in position, magically glued to your hand. Practice will show you just how far you can go in terms of turning your hand and shaking it.

11

YOU MUST BE PSYCHIC

The magician is able to detect cards that have been secretly moved by members of the audience.

*T*he magician lays out a row of eleven cards facedown on a table. He instructs a member of the audience to move any number of cards from one end of the row and place them at the other, one at a time. This all takes place while the magician has his back turned or while he is out of the room!

When the magician returns he moves his hand back and forth over the row of cards. Suddenly he stops at one card; slowly the magician turns over the card. The number on the card is the same as the amount of cards moved! The trick can be repeated immediately and as often as desired. In fact, the more often it is done the more baffling it becomes. At some point, a spectator will try to outfox the magician by not moving any cards at all. When this happens, the card turned over will be a joker!

THE SECRET:

Take from a deck eleven cards from ace to ten and one joker (any suits). Lay the cards out facedown on the table in the following order:

The Deepest Thought

The card at the right-hand end of the row is your key number. In this instance, it is a seven. Tell your spectator to move, one at a time, as many cards as he likes from the right end of the row to the left end. You can turn your back or leave the room. Let's suppose he moves four cards; the position of the cards will now be as follows:

10 9 8 7 6 5 4 3 2 1 J

Remembering that your key number was seven, move your hand back and forth over the cards as if to pick up magic vibrations. As you do this count to the seventh card from the left-hand end of the row and turn it over. It is a four. From this you have magically worked out that the spectator moved four cards. Try it.

It is now a simple matter of counting four cards along the row to the right from your key number four (4 3 2 1 J) to realize that the card on the right-hand end of the row is a joker. The J, which represents eleven, now becomes your new key number.

When you repeat the trick, all you do is count to the eleventh card from left to right and turn over that eleventh card. This card will tell you how many cards have been moved.

Some simple rules to remember:
1. This is a mathematical trick.
2. Always know the number of the card at the right-hand end. This is your key number.
3. After the cards have been moved, count your key number from left to right and turn up that card. This card denotes

the number of cards that have been moved by the specta-tor. As you turn it down again, mentally calculate which card is now at the right-hand end, because this will be your new key number.

4. If you turn up a joker, it means that the spectator has tried to catch you out by not moving any cards.

12

Card on the Ceiling— Version One

A chosen card is discovered attached to the ceiling

I like card tricks because cards are so common. Most people are familiar with them. In this trick, a spectator chooses a card. The card is returned to the deck and the entire deck is thrown up in the air. After the cards have fallen to the ground, one card, the chosen card, is stuck to the ceiling, facedown.

The secret:

Using any of the card forces explained in this book, force a card on a member of the audience. Once the card has been returned to the deck, move the chosen card to the top of the deck. If you like chewing gum, you will love this next bit. Have a piece of chewing gum in your mouth during this trick. Once the chosen card is on the top of the deck, you will turn and throw the deck up against the ceiling. When your back is to the audience, take the gum out of your mouth and stick it to the back of the top card (the chosen card).

Now throw the deck up against the ceiling. The chosen card will remain in place thanks to the gum.

13

CARD ON THE CEILING—
VERSION TWO

A chosen card magically attaches itself to the ceiling

Much like the "gum" version of this trick, a card is selected, the deck is thrown into the air, and the chosen card is seen attached to the ceiling.

THE SECRET:

This is the method used by many magicians. Before the show, when no one is around, get a card and attach it to the ceiling. Use a thumbtack, tape, or glue, making sure you will not be leaving any damage behind.

Force a duplicate of this card on a member of the audience. Once the card has been returned, throw the deck into the air. No need to worry about hitting the ceiling since a duplicate of the chosen card is already in place.

Do not tell anyone you plan to throw the deck into the air in order to find the chosen card. If you do, someone might look up too soon.

14

IMPROMPTU RISING CARD

Sometimes you need to do a trick at a moment's notice.
Here is a big effect done small and fast.

A card is chosen by a member of the audience, then returned to the deck. The deck is mixed and put back in the box. After a moment, the chosen card is seen to rise from the deck and out of the box.

THE SECRET:

Allow a member of the audience to freely choose a card. Once the card has been memorized, have him or her return it into the deck. Shuffle or mix the deck, all the while working the chosen card to the top of the deck.

The card box has been specially prepared with a small hole near the top on the back of the box. The hole is just large enough for your index finger to enter. When the cards have been returned to this box, it is simple to hold the box upright and with the tip of your index finger push the top card, the chosen card, up out of the box.

When the trick is done, return the card and put the box away. You don't want anyone seeing how this miracle was performed, do you?

15

BEHIND YOUR BACK

An impromptu card trick

A deck of cards is handed to a spectator who is asked to shuffle them. This spectator now asks another spectator to choose a card. Once the card is chosen and has been returned to the deck, the magician is able to identify the chosen card.

THE SECRET:

Any deck can be used. Hand the deck out and have it shuffled. Once the second spectator chooses a card, take the deck while the spectator shows the chosen card around for everyone to see except the magician. Place the deck behind your back, reverse the bottom card, then turn the deck over. The reversed bottom card gives the illusion that the deck is right side up. Actually, it is upside down. Turn your back toward the spectator with the chosen card and ask that it be slipped back into the deck. Be careful not to let the audience discover that the deck is upside down.

Once the card is back in the deck, turn and face your audience. Reverse the top card and place it on the table. Now the deck is faceup. Cut the deck a few times, then spread it out across the table. One card will be upside down—the chosen card.

16

CUTTING A CARD IN TWO

A playing card is cut in two, then restored

A playing card is freely chosen, then sealed in an envelope just large enough to hold the card. The envelope is cut into two separate pieces. The pieces are put back together, the envelope is opened, and the card is whole again. The envelope and the card can be inspected.

THE SECRET:

The envelope is prepared ahead of time with a slit in its middle. When you insert the card into the envelope, allow half of the card to slip out of the envelope. Seal the envelope and place it on the table. Pick up the scissors and explain that you will cut the envelope in two. As you pick the envelope off the table, curl the protruding card into the hand that is holding the envelope.

Cut the envelope in half allowing the top half (now empty, since you have the card slightly bent so it can be concealed in your hand) to fall away. Pick up the envelope that you have just cut and try to piece the two parts back together. Maneuver the envelope in your hand as you tear open the top of the envelope, then slip the card out. As long as you were careful to cut the envelope along the original slit, you can freely hand out both the card and the envelope for inspection.

17

THE DEEPEST THOUGHT

Locate cards by feeling them

*T*he magician takes out a deck of cards and asks a spectator to choose any twenty-one cards from the deck. Then the magician takes the leftover cards and puts them away. Next he takes the twenty-one cards and deals them left to right into three piles facedown. He then asks the spectator to point to any pile. He tells the spectator to look at the cards in that pile and choose a card, memorize it, and place the pile back where he found it. Then the magician picks up a pile that was not chosen and places it on top of the selected pile, and places the other pile that was not chosen under the other two piles. The selected pile, is now sandwiched between the other two piles. Next, he deals the cards left to right again into three piles facedown.

Then he asks the spectator to choose a pile and see if his card is in the pile. When the pile with the chosen card is found, the magician groups all the cards together again, sandwiching the chosen pile in between the other two piles. The magician does this three times and then sandwiches the pile again.

By this time, the magician knows that the chosen card is the eleventh card in the pack. He fans out the cards in his hand and asks the person to rub his or her finger along the cards, touching them all. Then the magician squares up the pack and tells the

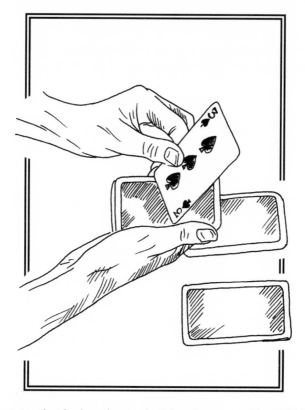

spectator that he is going to find the chosen card by ESP. He starts at the top of the pack and rubs the card. As he rubs them he throws them down and keeps count of what card he is on. When he reaches the ninth card, he puts it in another pile, saying that he got some "feeling" from that card. The tenth goes in the large pile, and the eleventh gets put with the ninth after the magician says he got something from that card, too. Now he just has to remember which card is the eleventh.

He will also find two more cards with that "feeling" and put the rest in the other pile. Now, the magician feels the four special cards again. He throws away the first, the second, and the third, which is the eleventh card. He must remember where he throws it. He then throws away the last card. He picks up the eleventh card, which he just threw down, and asks the person to touch it again, and afterward he flips it over to reveal the chosen card.

THE SECRET:

This a mathematical trick that always works. Follow the instructions carefully and you will see what I mean.

Thanks to Josh Morgan of Annawan, Illinois, for providing the idea for this trick.

18

THE LONG-STEMMED GLASS

Aces magically appear in a glass.

*T*he magician takes a long-stemmed glass and announces that he's going to perform a card trick. The thing about this card trick is that he will not be able to touch the cards because they will be inside the glass the whole time! Placing the pack face-out in the glass, the magician states that he's going to find all four aces using special "locator cards." He reaches into the glass and pulls out a red number card (we'll use the ten of hearts for the example) and puts it in front of the rest of the cards in the deck so that it is the card the audience now sees looking at them through the glass. The magician then states that he will let that red ten find a red ace.

Holding the glass by the stem, the magician passes a cloth napkin over the glass quickly. When the napkin has completed its quick pass, a red ace has replaced the red ten! The magician then takes the red ace and puts it in back of the deck and passes the napkin again. This time, the other red ace replaces the red ten!

Now the magician chooses a black number card (say, the six of spades) for the "locator card" and puts it in front of the red ten. A quick napkin pass, and there's a black ace! The magician takes the ace and puts it behind the deck. Another pass, and there is the second black ace! Now he pulls out the pack and puts it back in the box, smiling as he takes his bow. All of this magic occurs in the glass, so there is apparently no way that he could have manipulated the cards. When you perform the trick, people will fall down at your feet and worship your incredible abilities.

THE SECRET:

A slight amount of preparation work is required, but this trick is worth it. First, find a wineglass or any other long-stemmed glass that will allow you to set at least half a deck of cards in it (there can be no design on the glass or stem). Next, take the two red aces and glue them back to back. Make sure you make them look as much like one card as possible. Do the same with the two black aces. Now get two identical numbered cards—one black and one red—from an identically backed deck.

Next, glue one red and one black card back to back. Finally, get a cloth napkin that is big enough and dark enough to completely cover the glass. With this prep, you are set!

SET UP THE DECK AS FOLLOWS:

Set the black six-card faceup on top of the facedown deck. Now set the double-sided black ace on top of it. Now place the double-sided red ten/black six card with the red ten faceup. Next come the double-sided red aces. And finally, the last red ten *facedown* on the facedown deck. The rest is showmanship.

Place the deck in the glass with the bottom card facing your spectators. Announce that you are going to do the trick using a red "locator card." Pull the red ten off the top of the deck and put it on the bottom, facing the spectators. You should now be looking at a red ace. Holding the glass by the stem, you pass the napkin over the glass and spin it around so that the ace is now facing the spectator. It helps if you rigidly hold the glass with your fingers and the stem in the first bend of your finger. When you spin the glass, your thumb does the work and your fingers look much the same. Now take the ace and put it on top of the deck.

You should now be looking at the other red ace. Perform the pass/spin again, and your spectators see the other red ace. Now say that you need a black "locator card." Take the red/black card off the top with the six facing the spectator. Put it on the bottom of the deck. You should now be looking at a black ace. Pass/spin and your spectators see it. Take it, put it on top of the deck, and perform the pass/spin. There is the final black ace! Now merely put the deck back into its box before anyone gets too close.

When you get to the black aces, if you stick the ace of spades on top, so that it is the first ace you will show, you can ask the spectators to name a black ace. Nine out of ten times, they will say the ace of spades! You then make it appear for them. If they happen to mention the ace of clubs, just say, "So that leaves the ace of spades," and make it appear.

Thanks to Liran at shaolin@internet-zahav.net for the idea for this great trick!

19

THE RESTORED CARD TRICK

The jigsaw puzzle that puts itself back together

*Y*ou show two small empty matchboxes. Someone chooses a card from your pack. "I'm going to make a jigsaw puzzle of your card," you explain as you tear it into four pieces. You put the pieces into one matchbox and turn the boxes over four times. Now, if the magic has worked, the card pieces have flown from one matchbox to the other. The puzzle has been solved because the pieces pulled themselves back together. Open the empty matchbox and show that the chosen card has appeared inside! Then you discover that one piece is missing. Open the other box, which held the original torn pieces. Except for one piece, the other pieces have disappeared from that box. Match the piece to the torn part of the restored card, and it fits exactly.

MATERIALS:

Two inexpensive, identical packs of cards; three empty matchboxes; scissors; pencil; ruler; and glue.

THE SECRET:

The "choice" of card is forced. A duplicate card, minus one piece, is carefully hidden inside one matchbox so that you can show that the box is, apparently, empty. The other matchbox has a divided drawer. Turning the box around switches the torn pieces in one end for the missing piece hidden in the other end.

To make the divided box, cut a drawer exactly in half and discard one piece. Take the other piece and trim one sixteenth of an inch off the top three edges. Then glue the half drawer, open end flush to the left, inside the bottom of the drawer from the third box.

Take any card from one pack. Put it on top and put the pack in your left pocket. Remove the duplicate card from the second pack and fold it in four. Tear out the top left quarter, somewhat raggedly. Fold the piece in half and put it the left end of the divided matchbox drawer. Push the drawer out a half inch to the right and put that box in your left pocket. Refold the remainder of the duplicate card. Take another matchbox and push the drawer

out a half inch to the left. Slide the folded card into the right end of the cover. Put that box in your right pocket.

THE PERFORMANCE:

"Please keep your eyes on this little box," you call out as you take the matchbox from your left pocket. Slide the drawer halfway out to the right, watching so as not to slide it beyond the divider. Shake the box upside down to show that it is apparently empty.

"And keep your eye on this one, too," you say, as you put down the first box with the half-open drawer opening to the right and take out the other box. Grip the partly open drawer with your left thumb and fingers, and hold the right end of the box with your thumb on top of the first finger up inside the cover, pressed against the hidden card. Keep the card in place by pinching it between your right thumb and finger, and pull the drawer three quarters open with your left hand. Shake the box upside down, close it, and put it on the right-hand side of the table.

Force the duplicate card on an audience member with any of the methods you find in this book. Tear the card in four pieces and show them to the audience, then put them in the left-hand box (which is halfway open) and close the box.

Take one box with each hand, turn both boxes over, and put them upside down on the table. Open the right-hand box, shake out the folded card, and unfold it. Pretend to discover that one piece is missing. Pick up the other box, slide the end open, and shake out the missing piece. Tell your audience, "I guess that piece just didn't want to go away."

Thanks to Hilberto Riverol of Belize City, Belize, Central America, for providing the idea for this trick.

20

WRONG-WAY CARD

A chosen card magically turns upside down in the deck.

This trick can be done quickly with any deck and at just about any time. Have a card randomly selected from a deck of cards. The chosen card is noted, then returned to the deck. The deck is turned upside down and spread across the table. The chosen card is found to be the only upside down card in the deck.

THE SECRET:

A card is freely chosen. While the card is being examined, unnoticed by your audience you turn the bottom card of the deck upside down. Then turn the entire deck upside down before the chosen card is slipped back into the deck. Make eye contact with your spectator. When eye contact is made, turn the deck right side up and remove the bottom card. "Is this your card?" you ask as you show the bottom card. Of course, it is not. At this point, return this card to the deck, turn the deck over, and spread the cards across the table. One card will be reversed. It turns out to be the chosen card.

ALTERNATE VERSION:

Once the card has been chosen, place the deck behind your back. While the deck is behind your back, turn the bottom card over and then turn the deck upside down. Turn your back to the audience and have someone slip the chosen card into the pack. (The pack is upside down but looks okay since the top card has been reversed.) When the card is safely back in the deck, turn and face your audience, with the deck still behind your back. Return the deck to the right side up position and turn the bottom card back. Bring the deck in front of you. Spread the deck out and the one card that is reversed is the chosen card.

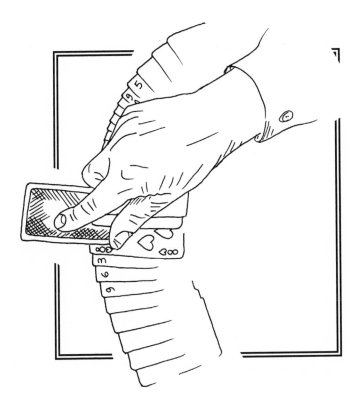

21

REVERSE PALM

Change a card with a sweep of your hand.

*T*his is one of my favorites. I have done this trick both on television and close up. It never fails to amaze.

The deck is in your hand. The bottom card is facing the audience. With your other hand, sweep down in front of the deck. Stop just for a moment and square the deck. Continue the downward sweeping motion. Amazingly, the card that was facing the audience just a moment ago is now gone and another card is in its place. All eyes immediately go to the sweeping hand. However, with a little flair, it is shown to be empty. You might even do this trick again, ever so slowly, with the same results.

THE SECRET:

When you put the deck into your left hand, keep a few cards in the palm of your right hand. The left hand is held chest high, bottom card facing out. The right hand is at your right side. Make mention of the bottom card, sweep your right hand over the left hand. When you stop to square the deck, leave behind the cards in your right hand. As your right hand continues on its downward sweeping motion, continue to keep your right hand in the position it was before delivering the cards into your left hand. In other words, you now want people to think that you have merely taken the bottom card off the deck and now are trying to hide it in your right hand.

Reveal that the bottom card has magically vanished. All eyes will go to your right hand. With a flourish—and a grin—show that this hand is empty.

Use a few cards to cover the bottom card. When you are asked to show the next to bottom card, you can.

Since magicians like to be fooled, show them this one. It is not too widely known.

22

READING THE ENTIRE DECK

Name each card of a deck while blindfolded.

*T*he magician holds the deck with the cards facing the audience. He then names each card as he peels it off the bottom of the deck.

THE SECRET:

Turn the top card faceup and hold the deck with this card facing your audience. It will naturally appear to be the bottom card. Name this card to them, at the same time noting the card that faces you. Put the deck behind you and transfer the card you have just noted to the "audience" side of the deck. Name this card, at the same time noting the next one. You can keep this up until the whole deck is named, one by one. This is more effective if you do it blindfolded, managing to read the bottom index of the cards, as they face you, by peeping under the blindfold.

Sometimes, the how-it-is-done part of a trick is so simple you might not think it would be effective. However, it can be. This trick is no exception to that rule. But naming the entire deck, even blindfolded, could become boring. Instead, reverse the top five cards after you turn the top card faceup (as instructed at the beginning of this trick). After these cards have been "read" you can move on to another trick. Alternatively, allow the deck to be examined.

23

VISUAL CARD VANISH

Making a chosen card vanish

Six cards are shown to the audience. The cards should be jumbo cards. If you want people in the back row to be able to see them, set up on an easel. The cards could also be displayed on a monitor or television screen, or on an Internet site. Ask that each person looking at the cards mentally make note of one card. Remove the cards. Have each member of the audience write down his or her card. Tell the audience that you know which card each member has chosen. You will remove the chosen card and put the remaining five back on the easel. When you put five cards back, each member of the audience will see that their card is missing.

THE SECRET:

Six cards are displayed; king of hearts, jack of clubs, king of spades, queen of diamonds, queen of clubs, and jack of diamonds. An audience member memorizes one card. Alternatively, ask all members of the viewing audience to memorize a card for themselves. Remove the cards. Tell the audience that you will mix up the cards and return five of them to view. The one card that has been removed will be their card.

Replace the cards. Only do not replace the originals. Instead, use the following five cards, which have been sitting on the table: queen of hearts, king of clubs, jack of hearts, queen of spades and king of diamonds.

Regardless of which card was chosen from the first group, it will be gone. None of the cards from the first group is displayed in the second group. Most people will be unable to recall which cards made up the first group. Most of all, they will be concentrating on their own choice.

I performed this very trick on television and had a great response from both the studio audience and the home viewers. The screen was filled with the first six cards, which were then removed. I asked that each viewer write down the name of his or her card. Then the screen was filled with the second group of cards. Every time, the chosen card was gone. It never seemed to miss the mark.

It is important not to let the first group of cards or the second group of cards remain in sight for too long. If you do, people might realize the secret, that none of the cards from the first group is in the second group.

This trick works well. It even fools people who see it on an Internet site.

My thanks to Adam Blechman for reminding me of this gem.

24

CARD IN FRAME

A card magically appears as a picture

A small picture frame is shown empty; a card is chosen, then returned to the deck. The frame is shown again. This time the chosen card appears in it.

THE SECRET:

Black glass. Buy a picture frame with a black inner lining (the inner lining is the cardboard below the glass, within the frame). I like black since a playing card can be seen better on this color surface. Buy a piece of thin glass, sized to fit into the face of the frame. Paint one side of the glass with black lacquer. Open the frame and place a card into the frame as if it were a picture (I would suggest using a deck such as the Svengali deck for this trick; take one of the many duplicate cards and put it into the frame). Best rule of thumb: The frame should be at least twice the size of the card.

Place the glass onto the frame. From a distance, when you hold up the frame, people are fooled into thinking they are looking at an empty frame. Riffle the deck. Once someone chooses a duplicate to the card in the frame, you are ready to perform this trick. Return the card to the deck. Put the deck away. Pick up the frame, being careful to hold the glass in place, and cover it with a large scarf. Now lean the frame forward onto the scarf. The glass will secretly fall onto the scarf. Lift the frame away from the scarf and voilà, the card is revealed, trapped in the frame.

You can even hand out the frame to prove that the card is in there and that it must have been trapped by magic.

This once was a regular in my act—until one of my assistants dropped the glass on the floor and it broke into fifteen pieces. I never did the trick after that. This trick really plays big. It's good for TV, stage, or a small platform. If you buy two frames, the ones with the very shiny inner black cardboard, you might be able to pull off this trick without the use of a false glass. Simply remove the inner cardboard from one frame, cut it down a bit, and use it in place of the glass. It might just work. Moreover, you will not have to worry about breakage.